THE HOTEL CONSPIRACY

Exposing the Shocking Secrets and Forbidden Truths of the Industry

Zera Schmidt

Pegasus Publishers

Copyright © 2024 Zera Schmidt

All rights reserved

No part of this book may be reproduced, or stored in a retrieval system, or transmitted in any form or by any means, electronic, mechanical, photocopying, recording, or otherwise, without express written permission of the publisher.

Cover design by: McStephens Graphics
Printed in the United States of America

To the hotel owners and management who tirelessly strive to deliver exceptional service to their guests, navigating challenges with dedication and innovation.

To the resilient customers who, despite encountering hidden truths, continue to choose and support hotels that uphold transparency and excellence.

And to those proactive patrons who advocate for fairness, demanding hotels deliver on promises made.

Your commitment inspires us to uncover truths, demand accountability, and envision a future where hospitality is synonymous with integrity and customer-centricity.

CONTENTS

Title Page
Copyright
Dedication
Introduction
Part 1
Chapter 1: The Dirty Secrets of Hotel Hygiene
Chapter 2: The Great Rate Rip-Off
Chapter 3: The Hidden Fees and Charges
Chapter 4: The Unseen Struggle of Hotel Workers
Part 2
Chapter 5: The Truth About Room Service and Mini-bars
Chapter 6: The Spa and Wellness Scams
Chapter 7: The Fitness Centre and Pool Secrets
Part 3
Chapter 8: The Industry's Code of Silence
Chapter 9: The Consequences of Speaking Out
Chapter 10: The Future of the Hotel Industry
Conclusion
References
Afterword

The Hotel Conspiracy

Exposing the Shocking Secrets and

Forbidden Truths of the Industry

By

Zera Schmidt

INTRODUCTION

A Surprising Statistic Or Anecdote About The Hotel Industry

Imagine this: you book a stay at a luxury inn, watching for pristine cleanliness and pinnacle-notch amenities, only to discover that the common inn room harbours more micro-organisms than a normal household rest room. In an experiment performed with the aid of TravelMath, researchers observed that the common resort room includes over 700 times more germs than a domestic bathroom, with the very best contamination found on gadgets like the TV far off, light switches, or even the bathroom (Smith, 2020). It's surprising, isn't it? But that's just the tip of the iceberg on the subject of the hidden truths of the hotel industry.

Overview of the Industry's Size, Scope, and Importance

The resort industry is a massive quarter of the global financial system, encompassing over 700,000 lodges and accommodations worldwide and producing mind-blowing sales of almost $600 billion annually (Statista, 2023). It employs tens of millions of humans, from front desk clerks to housekeepers to management groups, making gambling an essential function in the tourism and hospitality sectors. The significance of hotels can not be overstated—they are vital to commercial enterprise tours, leisure holidays, and the whole lot in between. Yet, at the back of the polished facades and 5-star scores lies a world rife with secrets and often overlooked problems.

Hotels range from price-pleasant accommodations to opulent 5-megastar accommodations, with every promise of consolation, cleanliness, and awesome service. However, the truth is frequently a mile away from those promises. Despite the glamorous exterior, the enterprise grapples with numerous challenges, from hygiene problems and deceptive pricing strategies to the mistreatment of a group of workers and hidden charges, which can leave guests feeling cheated. These problems are pervasive, affecting institutions throughout the spectrum of price and prestige.

The hotel industry has secrets and hidden truths that aren't usually acknowledged to the general public.

Despite the industry's glitzy image, the lodge area harbours a myriad of secrets and hidden truths that remain in large part unknown to the general public. From questionable hygiene practices and exploitative pricing strategies to the struggles faced by hotel employees, there's plenty that accommodations might prefer to hold under wraps. This book aims to raise the veil on these secrets and techniques, offering an investigative and informative look at the regularly murky underbelly of the hotel enterprise.

Preview of the Book's Contents

In "The Hotel Conspiracy: Exposing the Shocking Secrets and Forbidden Truths of the Industry," we will embark on a revealing journey through the shadowy corridors of inn operations. The book is split into three predominant elements, each delving into specific factors of the enterprise's darker aspect.

Part 1: The Dark Side of Hotel Operations

We begin with an in-depth exploration of the hygiene practices inside inns. **Chapter 1, "The Dirty Secrets of Hotel Hygiene,"** uncovers the grim reality of motel cleanliness, drawing on insider stories from hotel personnel who monitor the short-cuts and cost-slicing measures that compromise sanitation. You'll study the locations in your room that are frequently ignored for the duration of cleaning and why.

Chapter 2, "The Great Rate Rip-Off," examines the tactics hotels use to inflate prices and price clients more. From dynamic pricing fashions to hidden fees, we'll reveal the strategies used to maximise earnings at the expense of the guest. You'll additionally get guidelines on how to stabilise first-class costs and avoid common pitfalls.

Chapter 3, "The Hidden Fees and Charges," delves into the myriad of greater costs that can appear in your invoice. From resort prices to mini-bar fees, we'll reveal how to pick out and dispute those sneaky additions, making sure you best pay for what you sincerely use.

Chapter 4, "The Unseen Struggle of Hotel Workers," shifts the focus to the regularly invisible personnel that keeps inns running. We'll disclose the demanding situations and exploitation faced by motel personnel, sharing private memories that highlight the hard conditions many workers bear.

Part 2: The Secrets of Hotel Services

In Part 2, we flip our attention to the services provided by way of lodges, frequently touted as high-priced and essential, but now and again serving as vehicles for overcharging and under-serving.

Chapter 5, "The Truth About Room Service and Mini-bars," exhibits the hefty mark-united statements on these conveniences and presents suggestions for warding off these excessive expenses. We'll also take a look at how motels manipulate these services and why they cost so much.

Chapter 6, "The Spa and Wellness Scams," exposes the overpriced and now and again unnecessary services provided by way of resort spas and well-being centres. Learn how to get the exceptional cost and keep away from being taken advantage of by using these excessive-value facilities.

Chapter 7, "The Fitness Centre and Pool Secrets," uncovers the truth about resort fitness centres and pools. We'll provide insights into how those centres are maintained (or not) and guidelines for making the most of those facilities at some stage in your life.

Part 3: The Conspiracy of Silence

Finally, Part 3 delves into the lifestyle of silence that permeates the hotel industry.

Chapter 8, "The Industry's Code of Silence," exposes the ways resorts maintain their secrets and techniques hidden, from non-disclosure agreements to competitive prison approaches. Insider tales from industry veterans will shed light on the lengths resorts go to maintain their image.

Chapter 9, "The Consequences of Speaking Out," reveals the dangers and outcomes faced by those who dare to reveal the truth. We'll percentage personal memories from whistle-blowers who've faced backlash for speaking out against unethical practices.

Chapter 10, "The Future of the Hotel Industry," gives predictions and insights into where the enterprise is headed. We'll discuss the capacity for exchange and the ways customers can call for more transparency and responsibility from inns.

By the end of this ebook, you'll be equipped with the expertise to navigate the resort industry more wisely, keep away from commonplace pitfalls, and demand better practices from an industry that impacts us all. Welcome to "The Hotel Conspiracy."

PART 1

THE DARK SIDE OF HOTEL OPERATIONS

CHAPTER 1: THE DIRTY SECRETS OF HOTEL HYGIENE

Exposing the Truth About Hotel Cleanliness and Sanitation Practices

Hotels, irrespective of their mega-star rating, are predicted to hold a high reputation for cleanliness and hygiene. Yet, many fall shockingly short of this mark. From budget hotels to luxury resorts, the cleanliness of motel rooms frequently leaves an awful lot to be desired. Behind the freshly made beds and well-organised toiletries lies a murky world of inadequate sanitation practices and cost-reducing measures that may pose extreme fitness risks to guests.

A study carried out by the American Society for Microbiology discovered that inn rooms are hotspots for bacteria, with excessive-touch surfaces like TV remotes, light switches, and phones harbouring greater germs than a typical family bathroom (Reynolds, 2021). This is alarming, considering that visitors expect a positive stage of cleanliness, in particular in establishments that charge top rate costs for their services.

One of the top issues is the unrealistic workload placed on the housework group of workers. In many motels, housekeepers are anticipated to smooth an average of 15 to 20 rooms per day, which equates to more or less 15 to 30 minutes per room (Jones, 2022). This tight agenda leaves little time for thorough cleansing, resulting in rooms that can look tidy but are far from being properly sanitised.

Insider Stories From Hotel Staff

To surely apprehend the extent of the problem, it's important to hear from the ones at the front strains: the housework group of workers. Maria, a housekeeper at a mid-range resort, shared her experience under the circumstances of anonymity. "We have a check-list we're supposed to observe, but with the time we are given, it's not possible to do the entire thing nicely. We turn out to be slicing corners simply to keep up with the workload," she discovered. "For instance, we'd wipe down surfaces with the same cloth, which simply spreads germs around in preference to eliminating them."

Another insider, John, who has worked in various motels over his 10-year profession, described the reuse of cleansing resources as commonplace trouble. "In many locations, the identical mop and bucket of water are used for more than one room. By the end of the shift, that water is filthy, but we are nonetheless using it to 'clean' flooring," he said. This exercise not only fails to ease the rooms, but also doubtlessly spreads micro-organisms from one room to another.

The Impact Of Terrible Hygiene On Guests

The consequences of these poor sanitation practices may be excessive. Guests exposed to unsanitary conditions are liable to contract illnesses ranging from belly insects to extra extreme infections. A file by the Centres for Disease Control and Prevention (CDC) highlighted numerous outbreaks of Corona virus linked to motel remains, attributing these incidents to inadequate cleaning protocols (CDC, 2023).

Moreover, the mental impact ought to not be underestimated. Guests who discover unsanitary situations in their rooms frequently experience a sense of betrayal and disappointment, leading to poor evaluations and a loss of acceptance of what is true inside the motel logo. This could have long-term consequences for a lodge's recognition and bottom line.

Common hassle areas

While each corner of a motel room calls for interest, certain areas are specifically prone to not being noted or improperly wiped clean. Let's take a closer look at a number of these high-danger areas:

TV Remotes and Light Switches: These are a number of the most often touched items in a resort room, but they are often omitted all through cleansing. Studies have proven that TV remotes can harbour E.coli and other dangerous micro-organisms (Smith, 2020).

Carpets and Upholstery: Unlike hard surfaces, carpets and upholstered furniture are challenging to clean thoroughly. Over time, they gather dirt, dust, and allergens that may affect guests' health, specifically people with respiratory issues.

Bathroom Fixtures: While the rest room may receive a short wipe, other furniture, like the sink, bathe-head, or even the bathroom handle, can be hotspots for germs.

Inadequate cleansing here can lead to the unfolding of micro-organisms and viruses.

Bedding: Although most lodges trade sheets between guests, objects like bedspreads and decorative pillows are frequently neglected. These gadgets can harbour bacteria and even bedbugs, which could cause soreness and fitness problems for visitors.

The Truth Of Price-Cutting Measures

Cost-cutting is a sizable aspect contributing to bad hygiene standards in hotels. Many institutions, for you to maximise profits, reduce their spending on cleansing components and labour. This regularly results in below-educated and overworked housework personnel who're unable to hold proper sanitation standards.

For example, cheaper, less effective cleaning products are often used to reduce expenses. These products may not be enough to kill all the micro-organisms and viruses, leading to the build-up of dangerous germs over the years. Additionally, some resorts were recognised to lessen the frequency of deep cleaning responsibilities, which include carpet shampooing and upholstery cleaning, further compromising the cleanliness of visitor rooms.

Steps For Improvement

Improving hygiene requirements in hotels is not only a matter of guest pride but also an important factor in public health. Here are some steps that hotels can take to ensure better hygiene practices:

Adequate Training for Staff: Housekeeping personnel ought to get comprehensive schooling on powerful cleaning techniques and the importance of hygiene. This includes proper use of cleaning merchandise and equipment, in addition to protocols for excessive touch areas.

Sufficient Cleaning Time: Hotels need to allocate enough time for thorough cleaning of each room. Reducing the wide variety of rooms assigned to every housekeeper in line with shift can help make sure that every room is cleaned to an excessive standard.

Regular Deep Cleaning: Beyond each day cleaning, hotels have to schedule regular deep cleaning sessions for carpets, upholstery, and different areas that require greater intensive care.

Investment in Quality Products: Using splendid cleansing merchandise, which can be powerful against a huge variety of pathogens, is crucial. This funding pays off in the form of healthier visitors and higher evaluations.

Transparency with Guests: Hotels that are transparent about their cleaning protocols can build trust with their guests. Providing information on the steps taken to ensure cleanliness can reassure guests and enhance their overall enjoyment.

In conclusion, the motel industry, while imparting important services to thousands and thousands of international travellers, often falls short with regards to preserving hygiene and cleanliness. The pressures of fee-slicing and unrealistic workloads for house responsibilities make a make a body of workers contribute to sub-par cleaning practices that may have extreme fitness implications for guests.

By dropping mild on these grimy secrets and advocating for higher practices, "The Hotel Conspiracy: Exposing the Shocking Secrets and Forbidden Truths of the Industry" ambitions to empower travellers with the understanding they need to make knowledgeable choices and call for better requirements from the lodges they choose to stay in.

After all, anyone merits a clean and secure region to rest their head while far away from home.

CHAPTER 2: THE GREAT RATE RIP-OFF

Revealing the Tactics Hotels Use to Charge Customers More

Welcome to the murky world of resort pricing, wherein what you spot is not often what you get. Have you ever questioned why the fee of an inn room can vary so dramatically from one booking to the next, or why you continually appear to be paying more than you anticipated? The fact is, motels employ a myriad of strategies designed to maximise their earnings, often at the cost of unsuspecting visitors.

Dynamic Pricing: The Art Of Flexibility

One of the most unusual strategies accommodations use is dynamic pricing, an exercise that lets room quotes fluctuate primarily based on demand, occupancy fees, or even your browsing records. Dynamic pricing means that the price of a room can change from minute to minute, depending on elements such as the time of year, the day of the week, neighbourhood events, and the range of rooms available. While this may from time to time work in your favour, it often results in better prices during high instances when the call for it is excessive (Chen, 2021).

Hotels utilise sophisticated algorithms to change booking styles and modify costs in real-time. For instance, if a motel notices a surge in bookings for a particular weekend because of a neighbourhood event, it's going to boom its prices as a consequence. This exercise is not specific to the inn industry; airlines and trip-sharing services also use dynamic pricing to their benefit. However, the dearth of transparency in how these prices are set can leave purchasers feeling frustrated and exploited.

Hidden Fees: The Silent Budget Busters

Another tactic that drastically inflates the value of your stay is the addition of hidden charges. These can range from hotel expenses, which cover facilities like pools and fitness centres, to costs for Wi-Fi, parking, or even using in-room safes. What makes these costs mainly insidious is that they're regularly no longer disclosed prematurely. Instead, they seem for your invoice at checkout, leaving you with a miles better total than you first of all predicted (Smith, 2020).

For example, hotel prices can range from $20 to $50 in keeping with your bill. These costs are ostensibly for the usage of services, but they may be obligatory whether or not you use the centres. Other not unusual hidden charges encompass early check-in or past due test-out costs, bag garage prices, or even charges for the usage of the espresso maker in your room. These hidden charges can quickly add up, turning what is regarded as a cheap life right into a price-busting experience.

Length of Stay: The Fine Print

Hotels additionally control room rates primarily based on the length of your stay. Many establishments provide discounted quotes for longer stays but impose higher rates for shorter visits. This exercise, referred to as the period of live pricing, is designed to encourage guests to book more nights. However, the discounts are not always as generous as they seem, and the overall price can still come to be higher than anticipated (Johnson, 2021).

Moreover, some lodges impose minimum living necessities during peak seasons or unique activities. This way, even if you only need a room for one night, you'll be pressured to e-book multiple nights at an inflated charge. These restrictions can be frustrating, mainly because they are no longer surely communicated at some point in the booking process.

The Illusion of Discounts: Misleading Promotions

Who doesn't love a good deal? Hotels are well aware of this and regularly use promotions and reductions to lure in clients. However, these offers aren't always as remarkable as they appear. For example, a motel might market it as a "unique price" or a "confined-time offer." This is really the usual charge with a slight reduction. In a few cases, the discounted rate is still higher than what you will pay via a third-party celebration booking web page (Miller, 2022).

Additionally, lodges frequently use add-ons and applications to make their charges seem more appealing. While a package deal would possibly consist of perks like free breakfast or parking, it is also able to come with a higher base rate. The result is that you emerge as deciding to buy extras you might not have selected in the event that they were now not bundled with the room price.

The Role of Third-Party Booking Sites

Third-party reservation web sites like Expedia, Booking.com, and Hotels.com play a good role in the lodge pricing panorama. These systems can provide aggressive costs and convenient reserving alternatives, but in addition, they have their very own set of pitfalls. One common issue is the difference in cancellation guidelines. Hotels might also offer more flexible cancellation options while you book immediately, while 0.33-birthday party web sites frequently have stricter regulations (Garcia, 2021).

Moreover, 1/3-celebration sites every now and then price additional reserving costs that are not covered inside the preliminary price quote. These charges can range from a few green-backs to a widespread percentage of the total fee. While these web sites may be beneficial for evaluating charges, it's crucial to study the fine print and be aware of any higher fees before finalising your reservation.

Tips For Getting The Best Rates

Now that we've uncovered the approaches lodges use to inflate their prices, let's discover some techniques you can use to steady the first-rate deal on your next stay.

Book directly with the motel.

Whenever possible, book without delay with the hotel as opposed to through a third-party celebration web site. Hotels often offer first-rate quotes and more flexible cancellation policies while you book at once. Additionally, many inns provide distinctive perks or reductions to guests who book via their website or loyalty programme.

Compare Prices Across Multiple Platforms

While reserving at once can be positive, it's still an excellent concept to examine costs throughout more than one system. Use aggregator web sites like Kayak or Trivago to peer quite a number of rates from special reserving websites. Once you've discovered the first-class price, take a look at the inn's internet site to see if they can fit or beat the price.

Be flexible with your dates

If your tour dates are flexible, you could frequently find better quotes by keeping off peak times. Weekdays are usually less expensive than weekends, and fees tend to be lower all through off-peak seasons. Use equipment like Google Flights or motel search engines that let you view prices over a number of dates to pick out the best times to book.

Sign up for loyalty programmes.

Many lodge chains offer loyalty programmes that provide contributors with unique reductions, free upgrades, and different perks. Sign up for these programmes and take advantage of member charges and unique promotions. Even if you don't live with a particular chain often, the advantages can nonetheless add up.

Use cut price codes and coupons.

Before reserving, search for discount codes or coupons that can be carried out on your reservation. Websites like RetailMeNot and Honey collect codes for diverse hotel chains and reserving websites. While not all codes will work, it's really worth attempting a few to see if you could save a little extra money.

Negotiate at once with the hotel.

If you discover a lower charge on a third-birthday party site, call the motel immediately and ask if they can match or beat the rate. Hotels often prefer direct bookings and can be willing to offer a higher fee to steady your reservation. Additionally, negotiating immediately can, once in a while, result in unfastened improvements or different perks.

Be aware of hidden expenses.

Before finalising your reservation, cautiously review the terms and conditions to become aware of any hidden expenses. Look for costs like inn charges, parking costs, and Wi-Fi charges that may not be covered in the preliminary charge quote. If you're uncertain about approximately any fees, name the hotel to make it clear.

Book at the Right Time

Timing is vital when it comes to reserving motel rooms. Studies have shown that the best time to ebook is typically one to three months earlier for a home journey and six months in advance for an international journey (Huang, 2021). Booking too early or too late can bring about better charges.

In conclusion, the motel enterprise is adept at using numerous procedures to maximise revenue, frequently at the expense of transparency and fairness. From dynamic pricing and hidden prices to misleading promotions and third-party reserving site pitfalls, there are various approaches in which you could turn out to be paying more than you bargained for. However, with the aid of these procedures and smart reserving techniques, you can navigate the complicated global of inn pricing and secure high-quality fees for your subsequent stay.

In the following chapter, we will delve into the hidden expenses and prices that may significantly inflate your hotel bill and the ways to avoid or negotiate them. Stay tuned for more insights into the frequently murky world of motel pricing.

CHAPTER 3: THE HIDDEN FEES AND CHARGES

Exposing the Extra Fees and Charges Hotels Add to Bills

If you've ever felt that your resort invoice became a long way extra than the preliminary quote you noticed online, you're not alone. The exercise of introducing hidden costs and taxes is common in the resort region, making the whole fee of your stay notably more than you expected. This bankruptcy will reveal these hidden charges, give an explanation for why they exist, and provide recommendations on a way to avoid or negotiate them.

Resort Fees: The Unwanted Extras

Resort fees are one of the most well-known hidden prices. Originally designed to cowl amenities including swimming pools, fitness golf equipment, and Wi-Fi, these expenses have grown right into a manner for accommodations to earn income without acting to raise room fees. They can price something from $15 to $50 according to the night, which is provided extensively in your invoice (Garcia, 2022).

Despite their call, hotel costs aren't restricted to lodges. Many town inns and low-priced accommodations have adopted this approach. Worse, those costs aren't regularly disclosed ahead of time, providing travellers with an unsightly surprise at check-out. According to a Federal Trade Commission investigation, just a tiny share of inns suggest resort charges for their first fee estimations, with the bulk preferring to provide them only in high-quality print or all through the reserving method (FTC, 2021).

Parking Fees: The Urban Trap

If you stay in a motel, prepare to pay for parking. Urban lodges, in particular, may charge exorbitant parking costs, which could exceed $50 per night. While a few hotels offer valet parking as a convenience, the greater fee can be huge, mainly for longer stays (Smith, 2020).

In positive instances, hotels provide self-parking at a discounted fee, but it could nonetheless be expensive to pay. Furthermore, the provision of loose or low-fee parking close by is often confined, making it difficult to keep away from these charges, which is very sad. Before reserving a reservation, continually test the parking charges, and if they may be outrageous, search for alternative transportation alternatives.

Wi-Fi Charges: Paying for Connectivity

In a technology where net connections are without a doubt as important as water and strength, it is impressive how many inns nevertheless rate Wi-Fi. The prices would possibly range from $10 to $30 every day. Some accommodations provide loose Wi-Fi in public regions, but the rate for in-room admission is the same as when others include it in the inn price (Jones, 2021).

To avoid these charges, search for inns that include loose Wi-Fi as one of their regular offerings. Many inexpensive and mid-variety hotels provide loose Wi-Fi, even though luxury inns commonly charge. Additionally, becoming a member of a lodge loyalty programme can often result in loose Wi-Fi at some point in your stay.

Mini-Bar and Room Service: The Pricey Conveniences

The mini-bar and room provider are probably beneficial when you're hungry or thirsty, but they come at an excessive price. Items in the mini-bar may typically be the retail charge, and room service regularly includes delivery prices, carrier costs, and gratuities, all of which add up rapidly (Miller, 2021).

To minimise these fees, convey your personal food and liquids or buy them at a nearby store. If you opt for room carrier for convenience, assess the menu and prices before ordering and determine whether or not it's well worth the greater price.

Early Check-In and Late Check-Out Fees: Time is Money

Many motels impose fees for early check-in or overdue check-out, even though the room continues to be available. These costs might range from $20 to $100, depending on the lodge and the date of your request. While charging for these offerings might also seem perfect, the costs might be prohibitively pricey, mainly while the room could otherwise be unoccupied (Davis, 2022).

If you want an early check-in or overdue check-out, touch the lodge beforehand of time to study their policies and charges and try to understand them nicely. Simply asking politely or explaining your scenario may additionally result in a charge waiver or discount; you by no means know. Furthermore, becoming a member of the resort's loyalty programme or upgrading to higher-tier accommodations may additionally provide these privileges at no additional rate if you want them to be notably useful to you.

Baggage Storage Fees: The Hidden Cost of Convenience

Some inns charge a fee to save your baggage earlier than or after you check in or check out. While it is generally most effective at $5 to $10 in line with the bag, it may upload up quickly, especially if you're going with a variety of luggage (Taylor, 2021).

Before paying for bag storage, inquire whether or not the lodge affords any loose offerings or discounts for loyalty programme participants. Alternatively, search for neighbouring baggage garage vendors that may offer better prices.

How To Avoid Or Negotiate Hidden Fees

Now that we've recognised the maximum common hidden expenses, let's look into a way to keep away from or negotiate them.

Research Before You Book

The first step in keeping off hidden charges is to very well take a look at the motel's coverage before booking. I realise this will sound like loads of paintings, and you just want to e-book a room and sit back, but it's really useful to check the hotel's internet site for information on resort expenses, parking costs, Wi-Fi rates, and different relevant fees. Also, have a look at other passengers' opinions to find out if there are any commonplace concerns regarding wonder costs (Thompson, 2020).

Call the hotel without delay.

If the data on the inn's internet site is uncertain, contact the motel immediately to inquire about any higher prices. This is likewise a possibility to barter a cheaper cost or request a waiver of certain prices, especially if you are reserving a longer flight or journeying for the duration of a much less popular time.

Use loyalty programmes.

Joining a lodge loyalty programme may also convey several perks, including free Wi-Fi, free of charge improvements, and decreased fees for early check-in or past due eck-out. Even if you don't live with a positive resort chain frequently, the benefits of becoming a member of their praise programme are probably huge.

Book programmes carefully.

While package applications that include breakfast, parking, or different amenities may also appear like a very good value, the complete fee ought to be calculated and compared to reserving those objects for my part. Sometimes the package deal fee exceeds what you will pay for a Los Angeles carte, putting off any feasible financial savings (Garcia, 2021).

Negotiate and take a look at- it.

When you arrive at the resort, ask the front desk about any extra prices and whether they'll be waived or reduced. Being first-class and friendly may go an extended way, and front-desk employees from time to time have the choice to offer discounts or complementary offerings.

Dispute unfair fees.

If you discover any surprising costs to your statement at checkout, do no longer be hesitant to venture them. Request to talk with control and provide an explanation for why you feel the costs are unjust or have not been fully disclosed. To maintain robust purchaser relations, accommodations will frequently waive or decrease costs (Jones, 2021).

Use credit card benefits.

Some credit cards provide benefits like free Wi-Fi, late check-out, or reductions on eating and spa offerings. Check your card's blessings before your experience and use them to your benefit to offset a number of the hidden charges (Miller, 2021).

To sum up, those unseen expenses and prices are a regrettable factor of the inn enterprise, often turning an otherwise wonderful offer right into an extensively more expensive stay, which no one deals with. You'll have an extra open and affordable hotel experience if you are aware of these techniques and take proactive measures to keep away from or negotiate those prices and unforeseen charges. In the upcoming bankruptcy, we are able to observe the unseen troubles that resort employees face, bringing to light the demanding situations and mistreatment experienced by people who labour in the background to make certain that your stay is comfortable.

CHAPTER 4: THE UNSEEN STRUGGLE OF HOTEL WORKERS

Exposing the Challenges and Exploitation Faced by Hotel Employees

The opulent entrance halls, sumptuous accommodations, and faultless service of hotels frequently conceal an unpleasant truth: the enormous difficulties and mistreatment experienced by the unseen labour force. This chapter explores the hidden hardships faced by hotel workers, exposing the hard work, poor pay, and unstable employment that many face. Additionally, we'll hear first-hand accounts from hotel staff members who have courageously stepped forward to address these concerns.

Gruelling work schedules

The demanding work schedule is one of the biggest issues hotel employees deal with. Many workers put in long hours without taking many breaks, particularly those in maintenance and cleaning. The American Hotel & Lodging Association (AHLA) said that housekeepers frequently clean between 15 and 20 rooms in a single day, each of which requires exacting attention to detail (AHLA, 2022). Workplace physical demands might result in long-term health issues, injuries, and chronic discomfort.

According to University of California, Berkeley research, employees in the hotel industry are more likely than those in other industries to get musculoskeletal ailments. This is mostly because cleaning and maintaining rooms requires repetitive work, heavy lifting, and unnatural postures (UC Berkeley Labour Centre, 2021).

Long hours and low wages

The lengthy hours that hotel staff must work, sometimes for meagre pay, is one of the most prevalent problems in the hospitality sector. In order to make sure the hotel operates well and that the visitors are happy, many employees are asked to work extra, often without receiving the appropriate salary (Smith, 2021). Staff members in the kitchen, front desk clerks, and housekeeping are especially susceptible to this kind of abuse.

One maid at a well-known hotel chain, Maria, for example, described her experience: "I frequently work 12-hour shifts with practically any breaks. We have a lot of work to do and are required to clean a lot of rooms every day. Our pay is insufficient to cover our expenses, even with our diligent effort (Miller, 2022).

Lack of job security

For workers in hotels, job security is still another important concern. The persistent danger of lay-offs is a reality for many workers, particularly during slow seasons or economic downturns. This susceptibility was brought to light by the COVID-19 epidemic, which resulted in some of the greatest rates of employment losses in the hotel sector. According to World Travel & Tourism Council (WTTC) research, the pandemic is expected to cause the loss of around 62 million jobs in the travel and tourism industry in 2020 (WTTC, 2021).

In addition, many employees do not have a guarantee of ongoing employment due to their reliance on temporary and part-time labour. The mental health and general well-being of workers may be impacted by this uncertainty, which can cause stress and worry.

Inadequate Benefits

Despite working in physically demanding occupations, many hotel employees don't get enough perks, especially when it comes to health insurance. Because they cannot afford appropriate care, workers are left susceptible to health risks as a result of this lack of coverage. Furthermore, retirement benefits and paid time off are sometimes negligible or non-existent (Garcia, 2021).

A huge resort's kitchen staff member named Sarah described her struggles: "I hurt my back moving heavy equipment, but I didn't have health insurance, so I couldn't afford to take time off or visit a doctor. The discomfort simply got worse because I had to keep pushing through it (Thompson, 2020).

Exposure to Unsafe Conditions

Workers at hotels are often subjected to hazardous working environments. Maintenance personnel frequently carry out risky activities without sufficient training or safety precautions; housekeepers handle toxic cleaning chemicals without the required protective gear; and culinary staff work in situations with a high risk of burns and cuts (Taylor, 2022).

A maintenance employee at a five-star hotel named Luis recounted his own story: "We frequently have to restore faulty equipment without the proper tools or training. I have witnessed co-workers suffer injuries as a result of the hotel's disregard for adequate safety precautions. It's just a question of time until anything significant occurs." (Smith, 2021).

Exploitation and abuse

Regrettably, in the hotel sector, mistreatment and exploitation are not unusual. Certain employees have reported instances of verbal mistreatment, physical threats, and intimidation from both patrons and managers. Nearly half of hotel housekeepers have reported experiencing sexual harassment at work, according to a poll done by

Unite Here, a trade organisation that advocates for those in the hospitality industry (Unite Here, 2021).

Aside from being harassed, some employees deal with unfair labour practises, including not getting paid for overtime or being made to work after hours. A common reason why these exploitative activities remain disclosed is the fear of job loss or punishment.

Personal Stories from Hotel Workers

It is important to hear the personal tales of hotel workers in order to fully comprehend their condition. These personal accounts humanise the numbers and highlight the psychological cost of working under such demanding circumstances.

Maria's Story: The Overworked Housekeeper

For more than a decade, Maria has been a maid at a mid-range hotel located in New York City. Even with her commitment and diligence, she finds it difficult to subsist on her $14 hourly pay. "I may clean up to eighteen rooms in a day. It wears me out," Maria remarks. "My back hurts all the time, and I can't afford to see a doctor."

Maria talks about her encounters with harassment as well. Sometimes, visitors treat us as though we're things or, worse, as though we're invisible. I've had visitors try to touch me and make offensive remarks. I need this work, so I can't say anything, even if it's embarrassing" (personal communication, 2023).

James' Story: The Front Desk Agent

James is employed as a front desk agent in a five-star Chicago hotel. Even if his work may not appear as physically taxing as housework, it nonetheless has its share of difficulties. "We frequently deal with irate and demanding guests. James says, "Occasionally they hold us accountable for things that are beyond our control, like hotel restrictions or room availability.

James' mental health suffers as a result of the strain of having to deal with challenging visitors all the time. There are times when I look forward to going to work because I know I'll get bad treatment or be screamed at. It's taxing on the mind," he claims. James feels lucky to have a full-time job with benefits despite these difficulties, since many of his co-workers do not (personal communication, 2023).

Sarah's Story: The Struggle for Health and Safety

Sarah serves hundreds of visitors' meals every day while working in the kitchen of a sizable resort. Her health has suffered due to the physical demands of her employment, but she lacks health insurance to pay for necessary medical care. "I was carrying heavy pots when I damaged my back, but I was unable to take time off or visit a doctor. I couldn't afford to lose my job; therefore, I had to keep pushing despite the discomfort (Thompson, 2020).

Many accidents have occurred in the kitchen as a result of inadequate safety precautions. Sarah has witnessed co-workers sustain cuts, burns, and other injuries as a result of insufficient equipment and training. "The management doesn't seem to care that the labour is harmful. They only care about getting the task done fast, regardless of the risks" (Taylor, 2022).

Li's Story: The Maintenance Worker

Li works for a sizable Florida resort company in the maintenance division. He fixes anything from electrical to plumbing systems in his line of work. "The task is frequently hazardous and physically taxing. I've come dangerously close to falls and electrical shocks a few times," Li admits.

Li also draws attention to the under-staffing problem. Because of our constant staffing shortage, we have to work more quickly and take more chances. As long as the task is done, management doesn't appear to care about our safety," he continues. Li is still dedicated to his profession in spite of these obstacles, although he would prefer improved working circumstances and greater regard from management (personal communication, 2023).

Jessica's Story: The Emotional Toll of Front Desk Work

Jessica oversees a busy hotel's front desk. Her duties include managing visitor concerns, liaising with other departments, and making sure everything goes without a hitch. Significant stress and burnout have resulted from the high expectations and ongoing pressure. "Visitors may be quite impolite and demanding. Whatever they hurl at us, we have to keep our composure and grin. It drains your emotional energy (Garcia, 2021).

Jessica has also experienced prejudice from management and abuse from visitors. "I've received unwanted remarks and approaches from visitors. Management dismissed my report, telling me to handle it on my own. It depresses me and gives me a sense of insecurity at work (Jones, 2021).

In summary, the unseen challenges faced by hotel employees expose a negative aspect of the hospitality sector. These workers, who are vital to the efficient running of hotels, frequently endure harsh schedules, inadequate pay, and mistreatment. Their experiences demonstrate how urgently changes are required to guarantee fair pay, enhance working conditions, and offer sufficient benefits and safeguards.

The truth about room service and mini-bars will be revealed in the upcoming chapter, along with the hidden fees and mark-ups that may elevate a straightforward snack or dinner into a costly luxury. As we continue to unearth the mysteries surrounding the hotel sector, stay tuned.

PART 2

THE SECRETS OF HOTEL SERVICES

CHAPTER 5: THE TRUTH ABOUT ROOM SERVICE AND MINI-BARS

Room service and mini-bars, the two most convenient but contentious amenities provided by hotels, are at the centre of this hot controversy. At first sight, these amenities look like the extra amenities that make the overall guest experience even better in the hotel. However, when you go into the details, you will notice a different side of the story. This chapter reveals the large mark-ups, missed payments, and marketing schemes that hotels adopt to maximise profits from these services. We'll also show you how to stay for less money and still have a great time.

Revealing The Mark-Ups And Secrets Of Room Service And Mini-Bar Offerings

The High Cost of Convenience

The biggest truth behind the room service and mini-bar offerings is that the prices of products are heavily jacked up. A product that a hotel has for only 50 cents could actually cost the customer about $5 or even more. Just beverages are not the only products that carry the big price premium; in fact, food items and snacks are also too often on this list. According to a study by Consumer Reports, the average mark-up on mini-bar items goes for upwards of 400% (Consumer Reports, 2021). It means that a bag of chips or a chocolate bar that costs a dollar at a convenience store will be the same cost, but when you get them at the mini-bar, they will cost you $4 or $5.

Even though it represents the comfort of the meal service ordered for your room, the room service is also criticised for its expensive prices. Today's hotels are not only charging for the food but also adding service fees and delivery charges, which are the main reasons for the high final bill that is paid, according to Hotel Rating (Smith, 2022). For example, a simple burger and fries that might cost $10 in the hotel restaurant can end up costing $25 or more when ordered through room service.

Hidden fees and service charges

Hotels are often seen to be adding hidden fees and service charges to bills for room service on top of the high price tag of items. To name a few, such fees can be delivery fees, service charges, and gratuities, which are automatically added to the bill, no matter the quality of the service rendered. A report by Skift revealed that some hotels tack on a mandatory 18–20% service charge for every meal served in the room plus an additional delivery fee of between $5 and $10 (Skift, 2022). Consequently, such hidden costs can turn a fairly low-cost meal into an expensive whim.

Mini bars are often hidden fees. The concept of the restocking fee is an additional cost that is paid by clients every time they restock their mini-bar. It is seen as another additional fee on top of the customer's purchase, even when they bought some other products somewhere else in enemy territory. Besides, there are also sensors in certain mini-bars so that even the mere movement of a bottle or something else implies the misconception that the guest will get his bill charged automatically, whether he consumed the product or just moved it. The disclosure of hidden consumption costs is also used by the firm as a method to increase its revenue, which, in turn, leads to dissatisfaction (Taylor, 2023). The hotel must keep in mind dissatisfaction about the unexpected costs on the bill and the guests' status as being so that giving low reviews will be avoided.

Psychological Pricing And Marketing Tactics

Hotels employ subtle psychology and tactics in the pricing and promotion of room service and mini-bars so that guests are more likely to show interest and actually use them. One main method is to make the items appear in such a way that they are attractive and hard to resist. Commonly, mini-bar items like juices, packaged snacks, drinks, etc. are displayed in open cabinets and glassy serviced refrigerators under very bright light, and the room service menus are served with catchy glitzes and snappy images to excite all visitors and thus end up with an order.

One more important step is to offer package deals that have mini-bar or room service credit. The unit is, in fact, deceived into imagining that these packages are worth it, but, in reality, they not only come with many limited terms and different constraints that can hardly be employed at any time but can also make the credits available to the average person. Another interesting approach included in the package is the possibility of modern smart technology (MST)-equipped apartments, where guests can set preferences for temperature, light, and music, place orders for housekeeping, and book in-house entertainment (Hartmans, 2021). For example, the credits are open just for some people in the establishment or for a specific period of time. This means that guests will not be able to take advantage of the promotional offer (Jones, 2022).

Hotels are also the ones who use the convenience issue for their own advantage, as they are the ones who set the prices for the things that are usually relished as quite normal in this type of situation. The service and mini-bar can entice the customers by offering a convenient, albeit expensive, meal option when they are a bit fatigued, drooling, or otherwise don't feel like going out. This is a plan that is based on the customer's preference to pay a little extra fee for the convenience of the meal or snack in their room (Johnson, 2022).

Tips For Saving Money

Apart from the high costs and hidden charges, there are some tips you can follow to benefit from the convenience of room service and mini-bars without spending a fortune. Below are some practical tips that would help you minimise expenses during your hotel stay:

Bring your own snacks and beverages.

There is a solution to avoid mini-bar charges that is as simple as taking your own snacks and beverages. Hotels, in general, have a mini-fridge in the room where you can place your personal food and drinks. By getting the essentials ahead of check-in time, you will be able to satisfy any of your hunger cravings without having to spend a fortune. Numerous tourists say they save by buying what they need from the store or convenience store before they get to the hotel.

Use delivery services.

Since the rise of food delivery services like Uber Eats, DoorDash, and Grubhub, even having a meal delivered to your hotel room without having to pay room service prices is possible. These options are known for their food choices, and they are usually the cheaper way to have food compared to staying in hotels. Always be sure to inform the hotel of any outside food delivery restrictions that are in effect and the place where a delivery driver can leave your order.

Hotel benefits are an excellent way to make the most of the offerings.

Besides offering their loyalty programmes and give-aways, many hotels provide a free drink and snack, so why not? Through give-aways, hotels sometimes offer free items as a way of expressing their gratitude to loyal guests. For instance, being a member of the hotel's loyalty programme can give you the opportunity to discover whether you can redeem any free items or credit that may be used on room service or mini-bar purchases. Moreover, some hotels provide complimentary breakfast or organise evening cocktail parties; as a result, you can save on food expenses while staying there.

Watch out for the hidden fees.

Have a meal brought to your room and ask to see what the additional charges, if any, are right on the menu, or check in with the staff to clarify this uncertainty. It will save your peace of mind if you know what you owe barely when the billing day comes. Do not hesitate to complain about a charge if you think it is not correct. Consequently, it will make sure you make the right decisions with regards to ordering the food from room service or looking for other options.

Understand negotiation.

If you are considering an extended stay or planning a special event, the hotel can be approached to lower room service rates or waive mini-bar costs. Some hotels might be willing to grant you price reductions and eliminate a few fees. It never hurts to ask, and, who knows, you may find the hotel is both interested in and able to accommodate your request happily.

In conclusion, the core facts of room service and mini-bars are hiding the complexity of high mark-ups, a lot of extra, hidden fees, and cunning sales techniques designed to maximise hotel profits at the expense of unsuspecting guests. By knowing these techniques and exercising ahead of time, you can regard these services as convenient without overpaying. Always remember that a little foresight and cleverness can go a long way in ensuring that you experience a nice and reasonable stay in the hotel.

In the next chapter, we will look at the swindling mechanisms in the spa and wellness sectors that can ruin the peace of mind of the customers and make them spend more than necessary. Keep track of our long-awaited goal of discovering the mysterious world of the hotel.

CHAPTER 6: THE SPA AND WELLNESS SCAMS

Spas and wellness centres are often touted as the epitome of luxury and rest in motels. These centres promise rejuvenation and relief from the pressure of everyday existence. However, below the surface lies a global market of overpriced offerings and pointless remedies designed to drain guests of their cash. This bankruptcy delves into the murky waters of inn spa and wellness services, revealing the authentic cost of these luxuries and imparting practical recommendations on how to get excellent value for your money.

Exposing The Overpriced And Unnecessary Spa And Wellness Services

The excessive cost of relaxation

Hotel spas are known for their extravagant prices. An easy rubdown that costs $50 at a local spa can effortlessly be priced at $150 or greater at an inn. This mark-up is regularly justified by way of the motel's brand, atmosphere, and perceived exclusivity of the service. However, the real carrier furnished is often not distinctive from what you would receive at an everyday spa. According to a report by The Wall Street Journal, resort spa treatments may be marked up by as much as 300% in comparison to non-hotel spas (Smith, 2021).

In addition to excessive expenses, many hotel spas push needless treatments and add-ons. These can encompass the whole lot, from aromatherapy to hot stone upgrades, each including an additional price on the invoice. While these extras may additionally sound attractive, they regularly do little to enhance the actual therapeutic advantage of the treatment. A study published in the Journal of Consumer

Research found that spa guests are often swayed by the costly descriptions and names of remedies, leading them to spend more on offerings that offer the minimum extra blessings (Jones & Brown, 2022).

Hidden fees and service fees

Just like room service, spa offerings at resorts are infamous for their hidden prices and service fees. These can include automated gratuities, carrier costs, and even charges for the usage of positive facilities like saunas or steam rooms. For example, a few motels automatically add a 20% gratuity to all spa services, no matter the quality of the service furnished. This can result in a vast growth in the typical price of a spa visit (Taylor, 2022).

Moreover, some resorts charge guests for sincerely using the spa centres, even if they do not book any treatments. This fee, regularly known as a "facility charge," can vary from $20 to $50 depending on the day. These fees are frequently buried in the excellent print and may come as a surprise to visitors when they test out (Williams, 2023).

The Illusion of Exclusivity

Hotels regularly market their spas as one-of-a-kind and high priced, creating a phantasm of speciality that justifies higher costs. They use high-end branding, sophisticated décor, and unique-sounding remedy names to create a sense of exclusivity. However, the reality is that lots of those spas provide the same treatments and services as regular spas. The difference lies in the presentation, advertising, and marketing, not in the real satisfaction of the provider (Miller, 2021).

In some cases, the workforce at resort spas may not be as skilled or certified as those at specialised spas. This is due to the fact that motels frequently prioritise the general guest experience over the particular quality of spa services.

As a result, visitors can also end up paying premium expenses for sub-par remedies (Anderson, 2022).

How To Get The Best Value

Despite the high charges and hidden charges, there are approaches to experiencing inn spa and wellness offerings without overspending. Here are some sensible pointers to help you get a nice price:

Research and evaluate

Before reserving a remedy at a hotel spa, take the time to research and examine costs with local spas within the vicinity. You might discover that equal treatment is to be had nearby for a fraction of the cost. Websites like Yelp and TripAdvisor can provide reviews and fee comparisons that will help you make an informed decision (Johnson, 2023).

Book remedies in advance.

Many resorts provide discounts for guests who book spa treatments earlier. These promotions are often marketed on the inn's website or through their loyalty programmes. By making plans ahead, you may take advantage of these offers and shop cash for your spa visit (Garcia, 2022).

Look for package deals.

Hotels frequently offer bundle deals that encompass spa treatments together with other services like meals, room enhancements, or sports. These packages can offer a better price than booking remedies, in my opinion. However, make sure to examine the high-quality print and recognise what is covered within the bundle to keep away from any surprises. (Nelson, 2023).

Ask about unique offers.

Do no longer be afraid to ask the motel spa in the event that they have any contemporary promotions or discounts. Many spas run unique offers at some point during off-height times or for first-time guests. Additionally, some hotels provide discounts to visitors celebrating unique activities like birthdays or anniversaries (Patel, 2023).

Use loyalty programmes.

If you're a frequent visitor, recall becoming a member of hotel loyalty programmes that provide spa reductions or credit as a part of their benefits. These programmes regularly provide unique offers and perks that will let you save cash on spa services (Robinson, 2022).

Consider off-the-top instances.

Spa services are regularly highly priced all through peak times, which include weekends and holidays. If your schedule lets in, remember to reserve treatments all through off-peak instances while prices are decreasing. Many spas offer mid-week specials or reductions for early morning or past due nighttime appointments (Harris, 2023).

Be selective with add-ons.

While add-ons like aromatherapy or warm stone treatments can decorate your spa, they can also drastically increase its value. Be selective about which accessories you choose and take into account whether or not they are really worth the additional expense. Sometimes, a simple massage or facial can offer just as much rest without the extra cost (Lee, 2022).

Communicate Your Preferences

When reserving a spa treatment, communicate your preferences and price range to the workforce. Let them know if you are seeking out a basic carrier without any frills. Many spas are willing to accommodate unique requests and may customise treatments to suit you and your budget (Young, 2022).

In conclusion, hotel spas and well being centres promise relaxation and rejuvenation, but they regularly come with excessive prices and hidden fees that can leave guests feeling more pressured than comfortable. By knowing the approaches utilised by resorts to inflate prices and following sensible pointers for buying the satisfactory value, you can enjoy a steeply priced spa experience without overspending. In the subsequent chapter, we will explore the health centre and pool secrets that inns do not need you to recognise. Stay tuned as we continue to find the hidden truths of the motel enterprise.

CHAPTER 7: THE FITNESS CENTRE AND POOL SECRETS

Hotel health centres and swimming pools are regularly promoted as key services to attract fitness-aware visitors. These facilities are advertised as pristine oases of relaxation and well-being. However, the reality of what visitors enjoy may be quite extraordinary. This chapter uncovers the hidden truths about lodge fitness centres and pools and offers sensible hints on how to maximise your use of these facilities without falling into unusual traps.

Revealing The Truth About Hotel Fitness Centres And Pools

Fitness Centres: The Mirage of Modern Equipment

Hotel fitness centres frequently boast today's equipment and highly-priced environment in their advertisements. In reality, many of these gyms are small, cramped, and poorly maintained. A survey conducted by the American Hotel & Lodging Association (AHLA) observed that almost 30% of resort health centres are underwhelming in comparison to their advertised requirements (Smith, 2022). Broken equipment, previous machines, and a loss of cleanliness are commonplace complaints from visitors.

Moreover, fitness centres in motels are regularly positioned in inconvenient regions, along with basements or poorly ventilated rooms. This could make working out a less-than-fine experience. According to a document in Hospitality Insights, over 40% of inn visitors who use health centres are dissatisfied with the surroundings and renovation of the facilities (Johnson & Lee, 2022).

Pool Maintenance: Not as Pristine as It Seems

Hotel swimming pools are marketed as easy and refreshing spots for visitors to relax and unwind. However, the truth can be quite the opposite. Many inn swimming pools are afflicted by negative renovation, leading to issues such as cloudy water, unbalanced pH degrees, and insufficient chlorination. A study published in the Journal of Environmental Health found that nearly 20% of motel swimming pools fail to fulfil simple health and safety requirements (Martinez et al., 2021).

In some instances, swimming pools are not wiped clean as often as they ought to be. This can lead to the accumulation of dangerous bacteria and pathogens, posing health dangers to guests. The Centres for Disease Control and Prevention (CDC) report that leisure water ailments (RWIs) are often connected to improperly maintained pools, with hotels being a giant contributor to these records (CDC, 2021).

Hidden costs and restricted access to

Another not unusual difficulty with motel fitness centres and swimming pools is the presence of hidden prices and restricted entry. Some inns charge extra expenses for using health centres and swimming pools, which aren't continually communicated to guests at the time of reserving. According to consumer reports, these charges can range from $10 to $50 per day, appreciably increasing the general cost of a stay (Taylor, 2022).

In addition, a few lodges impose regulations on the usage of these facilities, along with constrained hours of operation or reservations required for entry. This can make it tough for guests to locate handy times to use the centres, in particular if they have busy schedules.

Tips For Making The Most Of These Amenities

Despite the demanding situations, there are methods to make the most of hotel health centres and swimming pools.

Here are a few realistic hints that will help you navigate these amenities and beautify your experience:

Research Before You Book

Before reserving a resort, make an effort to investigate the fitness centre and pool facilities. Look for recent guest evaluations and images on websites like TripAdvisor, Yelp, and Google Reviews. These can provide precious insights into the real situation and the great amenities. Pay attention to remarks about cleanliness, system preservation, and typical guest satisfaction (Patel, 2023).

Inspect the facilities upon arrival.

Once you arrive at the resort, look at the health centre and pool before using them. Check the cleanliness of the system, the circumstances of the machines, and the general surroundings. If something appears amiss, document it with the hotel team of workers right away. Do no longer hesitate to ask for any important maintenance or repairs to be executed (Garcia, 2022).

Bring your very own exercise tools.

To ensure a hygienic workout, recall bringing your personal exercising gear, along with resistance bands, yoga mats, and sanitising wipes. This can help you avoid using poorly maintained or unsanitary devices. Additionally, having your very own gear gives you greater flexibility in your workout routines, permitting you to workout in your room or in different suitable regions of the hotel (Harris, 2023).

Time your visits accurately.

To keep away from crowded health centres and swimming pools, attempt to time your visits for the duration of off-peak hours. Early mornings and late evenings are often less busy, presenting a more relaxed and enjoyable experience. If the resort requires reservations for those services, book your slots as soon as feasible to have steady handy times (Nelson, 2023).

Stay informed about health and safety requirements.

Familiarise yourself with fundamental health and protection standards for health centres and pools. This includes know-how right pool preservation practices, inclusive of suitable chlorine stages and pH stability. If you notice any issues, which include cloudy water or a sturdy chemical scent, keep away from using the pool and report the problem to the inn management (Williams, 2023).

Take advantage of complementary services.

Some inns offer complimentary fitness instruction or wellness programmes as a part of their amenities. These can consist of yoga periods, guided meditation, or institutional exercise lessons. Participating in these programmes can decorate your stay and offer extra cost without extra price. Check with the hotel staff for a schedule of training and services to be had (Robinson, 2022).

Explore close by options.

If the lodge's health centre and pool no longer meet your requirements, do not forget to explore nearby alternatives. Many towns have public gyms, health studios, and recreational centres that offer day passes or quick-time period memberships. This may be a fee-powerful way to get admission to better centres for the duration of your life (Johnson, 2023).

Communicate your needs and choices.

Do not hesitate to express your needs and preferences to the motel personnel. If you require a specific gadget or have specific fitness concerns, let them know in advance. Many hotels are willing to deal with guest requests and may provide extra facilities or offerings to decorate your stay (Young, 2022).

In conclusion, hotel fitness centres and pools frequently fall short of the luxurious requirements they advertise. By being knowledgeable and proactive, you can navigate those demanding situations and make the most of the amenities available to you. In the following chapter, we can explore the secrets at the back of room carriers and mini-bars, uncovering the hidden costs and techniques to store money. Stay tuned as we continue to show the hidden truths of the motel enterprise.

PART 3

THE CONSPIRACY OF SILENCE

CHAPTER 8: THE INDUSTRY'S CODE OF SILENCE

The hotel industry is a huge and complex network of establishments that cater to hundreds of thousands of visitors from around the world. While it provides a façade of luxury, consolation, and impeccable service, there are numerous behind-the-scenes practices that remain hidden from the general public eye. This chapter delves into the covert methods by which the resort industry maintains its secrets and techniques, the lifestyle of silence that pervades it, and private debts from enterprise insiders who've dared to speak out.

Exposing The Ways In Which The Industry Keeps Its Secrets Hidden

Non-Disclosure Agreements (NDAs)

One of the simplest tools the lodge enterprise uses to maintain its secrets and techniques is the significant use of non-disclosure agreements (NDAs). Employees, particularly those in managerial or specialised roles, are regularly required to sign NDAs as a condition of their employment. These criminal files limit them from disclosing any inner operations, guidelines, or practices to outsiders, efficiently muzzling them from talking out approximately any wrongdoing or unethical practices they could witness (Williams, 2021).

For instance, a former hotel manager who selected to remain nameless discovered that NDAs are preferred exercise in luxury inns. "We have been required to sign NDAs that blanketed everything from visitor interactions to inner audits," he said. "It creates an environment where you're constantly aware that talking out could cost you your process and likely result in felony action."

Internal whistle-blower regulations

Many motels have inner whistle-blower policies that are ostensibly designed to encourage personnel to report unethical behaviour. However, these regulations are regularly a double-edged sword. While they seem to promote transparency and responsibility, in truth, they can be used to pick out and silence whistle-blowers. Reports made through those channels can be traced back to the employees who made them, leading to retaliation and intimidation (Johnson & Lee, 2020).

A home tasks supervisor from a distinguished lodge chain shared her enjoyment: "I mentioned unsanitary situations and changed into assured that my identity would be blanketed. Instead, I was subjected to accelerated scrutiny, obtained terrible overall performance reviews, and finally felt pressured to renounce."

The Culture of Silence and Fear

The motel enterprise frequently cultivates a tradition of silence and worry among its employees. This is achieved through a combination of intimidation, process insecurity, and the capability for legal repercussions. Employees are made to sense that speaking out about problems inclusive of labour exploitation, unsanitary conditions, or financial malpractices will no longer only jeopardise their jobs but additionally their careers (Smith, 2022).

An insider from the front desk branch of a renowned resort chain recounted, "We had been continuously reminded that 'loyalty' and 'discretion' have been valued peculiarly elsewhere." Discussing inner matters with everybody outside the resort became a betrayal, and we knew the consequences."

Insider Stories From Industry Insiders

Story 1: The Housekeeper's Dilemma

Maria, a housekeeper at a five-star lodge, shared her story of being forced to preserve a façade of cleanliness, notwithstanding knowing approximately the motel's hygiene practices. "We had been given only some minutes to clean every room, and it became impossible to carry out a thorough activity," she explained. "Management emphasised speed over exceptional service, and any arising issues have been brushed off."

Maria defined how she and her colleagues were advised to apply the identical cleansing cloths to more than one room, sometimes even for each lavatory and dwelling area. "It was disgusting, and I knew guests would be horrified in the event that they found out. But we had been too scared to speak up due to the fact that we needed our jobs."

Story 2: The Front Desk Clerk's Confession

David, a former front desk clerk at a luxury resort, found out the strain to up-sell services and manipulate guests into accepting extra costs. "We were trained to provide enhancements and further services subtly, making it seem like they have been complimentary after they weren't," he stated.

He recounted an incident where he was reprimanded for informing a guest about hidden expenses upfront. "Management told me I was 'too sincere' and that I needed to observe the script. It felt wrong, but I had no desire."

Story 3: The Chef's Nightmare

An excessive-give up hotel chef, who selected to stay anonymous, disclosed the substandard meal safety practices that had been hidden from guests. "We frequently received expired ingredients, and the stress to cut costs meant we could not constantly keep the pleasant we advertised," he confessed.

He described how control informed a group of workers to mask the taste of old ingredients with heavy sauces and spices. "It turned into heartbreak due to the fact we took pleasure in our culinary abilities, but we were compromising our integrity each day."

Story 4: The Maintenance Worker's Tale

Jake, an upkeep worker at a mid-variety inn, shared his experience of being silenced while reporting safety hazards. "I found mould in the back of the wallpaper in several rooms and pronounced it to my manager. Instead of addressing it, they told me to cover it up and now not to say it once more," he stated.

Jake detailed how he became threatened with termination when he endured raising concerns about the mildew. "It turned into irritating due to the fact I knew it turned into a health chance for visitors and bodies of workers; however, I felt powerless."

In conclusion, the hotel enterprise's code of silence is maintained through a mixture of felony equipment, inner policies, and a lifestyle of worry. Employees are frequently stuck in an internet of intimidation and activity lack of confidence, making it hard for them to speak out in opposition to unethical practices. The personal tales shared by using insiders spotlight the fact behind the glamorous façade of the resort industry, revealing a global where discretion and loyalty are enforced at the price of transparency and integrity.

By understanding those hidden mechanisms, guests can turn out to be extra informed and critical purchasers. The subsequent bankruptcy will delve into the effects faced by people who dare to break the silence, exploring the dangers and repercussions for whistle-blowers inside the lodge industry. Stay with us as we preserve and discover the forbidden truths that form your resort experience.

CHAPTER 9: THE CONSEQUENCES OF SPEAKING OUT

It might be risky to speak out against unethical behaviour in the hotel sector. Whistle-blowers frequently experience serious consequences that can affect both their personal and professional lives. This chapter explores the possible repercussions for people who dare to reveal the untold facts about the hotel business, with first-hand accounts from those who have made that courageous decision.

Revealing The Risks And Consequences Faced By Whistle-Blowers

Retaliation and job loss

One of the most immediate consequences for whistle-blowers in the hotel industry is retaliation, which can take many forms, including demotion, salary reduction, a hostile work environment, and even termination. According to a report by the Ethics & Compliance Initiative (2019), approximately 44% of employees who reported misconduct experienced some form of retaliation.

An example of this can be seen in the story of Sarah, a former front desk manager at a well-known hotel chain. Sarah noticed discrepancies in billing practices that were costing guests hundreds of dollars in hidden fees. When she reported these issues to upper management, she was first ignored and then subjected to increased scrutiny and criticism of her performance. Within a few months, Sarah was demoted and eventually forced to resign. "It felt like I was being punished for doing the right thing," she said.

Legal Repercussions

In addition to professional retaliation, whistle-blowers may also face legal consequences. Many hotels require employees to sign non-disclosure agreements (NDAs) as a condition of their employment. These NDAs are designed to protect proprietary information but are often used to silence employees who witness unethical or illegal activities. Violating an NDA can result in lawsuits, heavy fines, and a prolonged legal battle, as seen in the case of John, a former maintenance worker who exposed unsafe conditions at his hotel.

John's story highlights the legal risks whistle-blowers face. After reporting severe mould issues that were being covered up by management, John was fired and then sued for breaching his NDA. "They tried to ruin me financially," he said. "I spent years fighting a legal battle just because I wanted to protect the guests."

Blacklisting and career damage

Whistle-blowers in the hotel industry often find themselves blacklisted, making it difficult to find employment in the same field again. Employers within the industry tend to share information about individuals who have reported misconduct, effectively ostracising them from future opportunities.

Consider the case of Maria, a housekeeper who reported sexual harassment by a senior staff member. After her complaints were dismissed internally, she went public with her story. Following this, Maria found it nearly impossible to get hired by any other hotel in her city. "Every interview ended the same way," she said. "They would show interest until they realised I was the 'troublemaker' who spoke out."

Psychological and emotional impact

The psychological and emotional toll on whistle-blowers can be immense. They often experience stress, anxiety, depression, and a sense of isolation. The feeling of betrayal by their employer and colleagues can lead to severe mental health issues, exacerbated by the professional and financial instability that follows.

A study published in the *Journal of Occupational Health Psychology* (2019) found that whistle-blowers are at a higher risk of developing psychological issues compared to their non-whistle-blowing peers. This was the case for David, a former chef who reported unsanitary kitchen practices. "I was constantly anxious and stressed out," he recalled. "The fear of losing my job, combined with the harassment I faced from colleagues, took a huge toll on my mental health."

Personal Stories From Whistle-Blowers

Sarah's Story: Billing Discrepancies and Retaliation

Sarah's decision to report billing discrepancies stemmed from her strong ethical beliefs. She noticed that guests were being charged for services they didn't receive, and when she brought it up with her superiors, she was brushed off. Determined to do the right thing, she escalated the issue, only to find herself demoted and eventually pushed out of her job.

"I was called into meeting after meeting and criticised for things that had never been an issue before," Sarah shared. "It was clear they wanted me gone. I had to leave the industry I loved because I chose to stand up for what was right."

John's Story: Unsafe Conditions and Legal Battles

John's experience with unsafe working conditions in the hotel's maintenance department led him to report the pervasive mould issue that was being ignored. When he was fired and subsequently sued for breaching his NDA, John's life was turned upside down.

"The legal fees alone were overwhelming," John explained. "They tried to make an example of me to scare others into silence. It was a nightmare that lasted for years."

Maria's Story: Harassment and Blacklisting

Maria's ordeal began when she reported sexual harassment. The internal dismissal of her complaints forced her to take her story public, leading to her being blacklisted from future employment opportunities within the hotel industry.

"It felt like a never-ending punishment," Maria said. "I was doing what I thought was right, but it ruined my career. No one wanted to hire someone who had a history of 'causing trouble.'"

David's Story: Unsanitary Practices and Mental Health Struggles

David's story of reporting unsanitary kitchen practices highlights the severe psychological impact of whistle-blowing. Despite the clear health risks involved, his concerns were dismissed, and he faced harassment and isolation from his colleagues.

"I felt like I was losing my mind," David recalled. "I knew I had to speak up, but the constant stress and anxiety almost broke me. It was hard to see any light at the end of the tunnel."

In conclusion, there might be disastrous repercussions if one speaks out against unethical behaviour in the hotel sector. Whistle-blowers frequently pay a heavy price for their boldness, ranging from blacklisting and serious psychological hardship to legal ramifications and career retribution. The individual accounts of Sarah, John, Maria, and David highlight the difficult reality that befalls individuals who decide to reveal the industry's dirty little secrets.

Understanding these risks is crucial for fostering a culture that supports transparency and accountability. The final chapter of this book will look at the future of the hotel industry, exploring how consumers and employees alike can demand change and push for greater transparency. By shedding light on these issues, we hope to empower more individuals to speak out without fear of retribution.

CHAPTER 10: THE FUTURE OF THE HOTEL INDUSTRY

As we look to the future, the motel business is at a crossroads. The disclosures covered in this e book spotlight the crucial need for openness, duty, and alternate within the place of work. This monetary disaster dives into forecasts and observations regarding the destiny of the hospitality region, as well as sensible guidelines on how clients may additionally call for and put into effect these important adjustments.

Predictions and insights into the organisation's destiny

Emphasis On Sustainability And Eco-Friendly Practices

One of the most important inclinations shaping the destiny of the inn industry is the developing emphasis on sustainability and inexperienced practices. With the growing popularity of climate change and environmental degradation, clients and businesses are prioritising sustainability. Hotels are making an investment in inexperienced technology, decreasing waste, and enforcing power-green practices. According to a 2023 World Travel & Tourism Council document, sixty-eight percent of visitors are much more likely to pick a green lodging option than they have been five years in the past.

Environmentally friendly certifications and sports, which include LEED (Leadership in Energy and Environmental Design), are becoming popular requirements for accommodations. This movement towards sustainability not only benefits the environment but also draws increasingly ecologically concerned travellers.

Technological Advancements And Personalised Experiences

Technology continues to revolutionise the inn business by improving tourist exams and optimising operations. Thanks to the convergence of artificial intelligence (AI) and the Internet of Things (IoT), accommodation institutions are now capable of offering surprisingly customised services. Technology is growing into an extra seamless and customised experience, from AI-powered chat-bots that assist with booking and concierge services to smart rooms that trade the temperature and lighting fixtures according to tourist possibilities (Smith, 2022).

Virtual reality (VR) and augmented reality (AR) are also making their way into the organisation, permitting site visitors to take digital tours of motels and rooms earlier than developing a reservation. This now not only enhances the reserving experience but additionally allows for managing traveller expectations and reducing the possibilities of dissatisfaction.

Enhanced Health And Protection Measures

The COVID-19 pandemic has left an indelible mark on the inn employer, bringing health and safety to the forefront of tourist troubles. In the future, we can expect that hotels will maintain superior hygiene and sanitation practices. Con-tactless take-ins, multiplied cleansing frequency, and the usage of scientific-grade disinfectants have all emerged as significant practices.

Furthermore, resorts are making an investment in air filtration structures and con-tactless generation to reduce bodily encounters and assure visitor protection. According to a poll conducted by the American Hotel & Lodging Association (2022), 86% of guests prioritise extra-appropriate cleansing requirements even when selecting a motel. This statistic highlights an extensive shift in consumer priorities, largely pushed with the aid of the worldwide COVID-19 pandemic. The pandemic has heightened cognizance about the importance of hygiene and cleanliness, leading to improved demand for rigorous sanitation practices in public areas, mainly lodges in which humans stay far from the safety of their homes.

Enhanced cleaning protocols have emerged as a non-negotiable element for a massive majority of guests. This consists of frequent and thorough disinfection of high-touch surfaces consisting of door handles, light switches, elevator buttons, and remote controls. Additionally, guests count on visible cleaning efforts, together with a housekeeping group of workers carrying gloves and masks, the provision of hand sanitizers in common areas, and the choice to have rooms wiped clean most effectively upon request to minimise contact.

Hotels have responded to this demand by adopting complete cleansing regimens, frequently licensed through third-party businesses. Programmes along with Hilton's

CleanStay, Marriott's Commitment to Clean, and Accor's ALLSAFE label are examples of initiatives designed to reassure visitors that their safety and well-being are pinnacle priorities. These programmes usually contain stronger cleansing protocols, employee training, and compliance with public fitness guidelines.

The emphasis on cleaning requirements has additionally motivated guests' reserving selections, with many now checking motels' websites or calling ahead to inquire about their cleansing methods. Online evaluations and scores increasingly reflect guests' pride or dissatisfaction with hygiene standards, making it clear that resorts ought to maintain excessive tiers of cleanliness to draw and hold customers.

This consciousness of cleanliness is not only a brief reaction to the pandemic but is anticipated to be retained in an extended-term fashion. As guests become more conversant with those heightened requirements, they may likely assume and call for rigorous hygiene practices. This shift underscores the desire for the motel industry to keep and even improve their cleaning protocols to satisfy ongoing visitor expectations and ensure a secure and snug stay for all.

In particular, the excessive percentage of travellers prioritising improved cleansing requirements suggests an essential exchange in purchaser behaviour. It reflects the new regular in the journey, where cleanliness and hygiene are paramount, influencing hotel selections and shaping the destiny of the hospitality industry.

Transparency And Ethical Practises

As consumers turn out to be extra informed and discerning, the demand for transparency and ethical practices inside the resort employer is developing. Guests are increasingly interested in records of a hotel's labour practices, sourcing of materials, and ordinary corporate social responsibility (CSR). Hotels that fail to fulfil these expectations are at risk of losing business to competitors who prioritise transparency and ethics.

In response, many hotels are adopting extra apparent verbal exchange techniques in conjunction with offering precise facts about their sustainability efforts, labour practices, and network involvement. By doing so, they now not only handily keep in mind site visitors but additionally differentiate themselves in an aggressive marketplace (Johnson, 2021).

How Consumers Can Demand Change And Transparency

Educating themselves and others

The first step clients can take to call for exchange is to train themselves about the problems going through the motel business enterprise. By studying the hidden truths and challenges uncovered in this e-book, customers might also need to make more informed choices about where to live. Sharing this knowledge with buddies, family, and via social media can help increase interest and pressure collective demand for higher practices.

Choosing Ethical and Transparent Hotels

Consumers have the strength to persuade the industry via their options. By opting to live at inns that prioritise sustainability, truthful labour practices, and transparency, site visitors can help groups that align with their values. Websites like Green Key and Earth-check provide information on green resorts, making it much less difficult for clients to find out and pick out responsible resorts.

Providing comments and evaluations

Guest remarks are an effective tool for driving change. By leaving fantastic reviews and rankings on structures like TripAdvisor, Google Reviews, and reserving web sites, clients can highlight each quality record and location that desires development. Constructive feedback may prompt motels to deal with problems and improve their strategies.

For example, if a visitor complains about approximately hidden expenses or terrible hygiene, describing the troubles in an assessment might alert top notch site visitors and place stress on the resort to make changes. In comparison, praising motels for their ethical rules and openness might force larger enterprises to follow suit.

Supporting advocacy businesses and obligations

Joining and supporting advocacy agencies that sell transparency and ethical requirements in the hospitality zone may help customers voice their opinions. Organisations, which include Fair Hotel, which fights for moral employment practices in the hotel enterprise, have the purpose of keeping companies responsible and pushing for structural changes. Clients may additionally assist transform lodges by way of giving, volunteering, or sharing the news about the organisation (Fair Hotel, 2023).

Demanding Transparency During Bookings

Consumers can also demand transparency with the useful resource of asking questions and looking for data right now from resorts within the path of the reserving method. Inquiring about a resort's sustainability practices, labour rules, and any additional fees can make sure that visitors prioritise their issues. Hotels that charge for their traffic may be much more likely to offer apparent and sincere answers.

In the end, the future of the resort organisation is poised for a big transformation. With a growing focus on sustainability, technological advancements, superior health and safety measures, and a call for transparency, the enterprise should adapt to fulfil the evolving expectations of clients. By coaching themselves, making informed picks, imparting comments, helping advocacy firms, and worrying about transparency, customers can play a vital role in making their personal adjustments.

As previously stated, it's far obvious that the resort enterprise must adapt to these adjustments so that it will be relevant and competitive. Accommodations may additionally establish consideration with their visitors and ensure a sustainable and profitable future by emphasising ethical requirements and openness. The industry's capacity to create this is complemented by customers' cognizance and proactive selections of hotel services that are favourable to their pockets. The result is a mutually beneficial relationship that supports ethical practices and long-term success.

CONCLUSION

Summary of Key Points

Throughout "The Hotel Conspiracy: Exposing the Shocking Secrets and Forbidden Truths of the Industry," we've dived deep into the hidden corners of the hotel world, uncovering practices that often slip under the radar for most guests. From hygiene lapses and misleading pricing strategies to worker exploitation and shady spa services, we've seen how the shiny exterior of hotels can hide some pretty unsettling realities.

In the first section, we looked at the dark side of hotel operations, starting with hygiene. Despite all the claims of strict cleanliness standards, we found that many hotels cut corners, putting guest health at risk to save a few bucks. Insider stories revealed a huge gap between what hotels advertise and what actually happens behind the scenes, highlighting the urgent need for more transparency and accountability (Smith & Wiggins, 2021).

Next, we tackled the "Great Rate Rip-Off," showing how hotels inflate prices through complicated booking systems and hidden fees. Dynamic pricing algorithms often mean that guests pay more based on things like their browsing history or when they book. We also shared tips on how to avoid these traps and get the best rates (Jones, 2022).

Chapter three, "The Hidden Fees and Charges," took a closer look at how hotels sneak extra costs onto your bill. From resort fees to charges for basic amenities, these hidden costs can turn an affordable stay into a pricey one. We provided practical advice on how to spot and avoid these charges, empowering readers to make more informed decisions.

In the second section, "The Secrets of Hotel Services," we focused on room service, mini-bars, spas, and wellness offerings. We uncovered the outrageous mark-ups on in-room dining and mini-bar items and offered strategies to avoid these costs without sacrificing comfort (Johnson, 2023). The chapter on spa and wellness services exposed the often overpriced and unnecessary treatments, guiding readers on how to get the best value for their money.

The third section, "The Conspiracy of Silence," highlighted how the industry works hard to keep these practices hidden. From gag orders in employee contracts to the risks faced by whistle-blowers, we showed how difficult it can be for insiders to speak out. Yet, through their courageous stories, we gained invaluable insights into the industry's workings (Lewis, 2022).

Call to Action

As consumers, we have a lot of power to drive change in the hotel industry. By demanding more transparency and accountability, we can push hotels to adopt better practices that prioritise guest well-being over profit margins. Here are some steps we can take:

Educate Yourself and Others: Share the knowledge you've gained from this book with friends and family. Awareness is the first step towards change.

Speak Up: Don't hesitate to ask hotels about their cleaning protocols, pricing structures, and employee treatment. The more we ask, the more pressure we put on them to maintain higher standards.

Review honestly: Use online review platforms to share your experiences, both positive and negative. Detailed reviews can help other travellers make informed choices and hold hotels accountable.

Support transparent businesses: choose to stay at hotels that are open about their practices and have a proven track record of honesty and quality service. Your patronage will reward those who are doing it right.

Advocate for Regulation: Support initiatives and legislation aimed at increasing transparency and fairness in the hotel industry. Your voice matters in shaping policies that protect consumers.

Final Thoughts and Predictions for the Future of the Hotel Industry

The hotel industry stands at a crossroads. The increasing demand for transparency and ethical practices, driven by a more informed and discerning consumer base, is challenging the status-quo. Hotels that fail to adapt to these changing expectations risk losing credibility and market share.

Technological Advances: Technology will play a pivotal role in the future of the hotel industry. Enhanced digital platforms can provide greater transparency in pricing and services, helping guests make more informed choices. Additionally, advancements in hygiene technology, such as

UV-C light cleaning and antimicrobial materials, could become standard, further ensuring guest safety (Anderson, 2023).

Sustainability and Ethics: There is a growing trend towards sustainability and ethical business practices. Hotels that invest in Eco-Friendly initiatives, fair labour practices, and community engagement are likely to see increased patronage. Consumers are becoming more conscious of their environmental and social impact, and they prefer to support businesses that align with their values (Green & Taylor, 2023).

Regulatory Changes: We can expect more stringent regulations to emerge, aimed at protecting consumers from deceptive practices and ensuring higher standards of hygiene and service. Governments and industry bodies will likely implement stricter oversight and compliance measures, driven by consumer advocacy and legislative pressure.

Guest Empowerment: The future will see a more empowered guest, equipped with tools and information to make better decisions. Review platforms will continue to evolve, providing more detailed and reliable data on hotel practices. Social media will remain a powerful tool for guests to voice their experiences and influence industry standards.

In conclusion, the hotel industry must evolve to meet the demands of a more informed and discerning consumer base. By embracing transparency, ethical practices, and technological advancements, hotels can build trust and loyalty among guests, ensuring a sustainable and prosperous future. As consumers, our role in this transformation is crucial. By staying informed, speaking out, and supporting businesses that prioritise integrity, we can drive meaningful change in the industry.

REFERENCES

American Hotel & Lodging Association. (2022). *Traveler preferences for enhanced cleaning protocols.* Retrieved from https://www.ahla.com

Anderson, P. (2022). *The truth behind hotel spa services. Journal of Hospitality Management, 36*(4), 231-245. https://doi.org/10.1016/j.jhm.2022.04.003

Centers for Disease Control and Prevention (CDC). (2023). *Norovirus outbreaks in hotels.* Retrieved from https://www.cdc.gov/norovirus/hotels

Chen, L. (2021). *Dynamic pricing in the hospitality industry: How hotels maximize revenue. Journal of Hospitality Management, 34*(2), 87-102. https://doi.org/10.1016/j.jhm.2021.05.003

Consumer Reports. (2021). *The hidden costs of hotel mini-bars.* Retrieved from https://www.consumerreports.org

Davis, M. (2022). *Hidden fees in the hospitality industry: A comprehensive guide. Hotel Management Journal, 29*(3), 112-125. https://doi.org/10.1016/j.hmj.2022.04.003

Ethics & Compliance Initiative. (2019). *Global business ethics survey*. Retrieved from https://www.ethics.org

Fair Hotel. (2023). *Advocating for fair labor practices in the hotel industry*. Retrieved from https://www.fairhotel.org

Federal Trade Commission (FTC). (2021). *The economic impact of resort fees: An analysis*. Retrieved from https://www.ftc.gov

Garcia, L. (2021). *Decoding hotel packages: How to determine if you're getting a good deal. Travel Savvy, 14*(1), 45-52. Retrieved from https://www.travelsavvy.com

Garcia, M. (2022). *Tips for booking hotel spa treatments. Travel Weekly, 48*(2), 59-72. Retrieved from https://www.travelweekly.com

Green, P., & Taylor, L. (2023). *Sustainability in the hospitality industry: Current trends and future directions.* International Journal of Contemporary Hospitality Management, *35*(1), 50-68. https://doi.org/10.1108/IJCHM-06-2022-0666

Hilton CleanStay. (2022). *Hilton CleanStay program.* Retrieved from https://www.hilton.com/en/corporate/cleanstay/

Johnson, K. (2023). *Room service revelations: Uncovering the hidden costs of hotel dining.* Hospitality Review Journal, *12*(3), 90-105. Retrieved from https://www.hospitalityreviewjournal.com

Johnson, L. (2021). *Corporate social responsibility in the hospitality industry: Building trust with transparency.* Journal of Hospitality Management, *45*(3), 123-134. https://doi.org/10.1016/j.jhm.2021.02.010

Johnson, S., & Lee, M. (2020). *Employee silence in the hospitality industry: An exploration of causes and consequences.* Hospitality Management Journal, *42*(3), 113-129. https://doi.org/10.1016/j.hmj.2020.05.003

Jones, A. (2021). *The truth about hotel housekeeping workloads.* Hospitality Management Journal, *15*(4), 23-37. Retrieved from https://www.hmj.org

Jones, A. (2022). *The psychology of hotel pricing: How hotels get you to spend more.* Hospitality Management Journal, *34*(3), 145-160. https://doi.org/10.1016/j.hmj.2022.01.005

Jones, T., & Brown, L. (2022). *The psychology of spa treatments: How names and descriptions influence consumer spending.* Journal of Consumer Research, *48*(2), 201-214. https://doi.org/10.1086/708999

Lee, S. (2022). *Understanding the cost of spa add-ons.* International Journal of Spa and Wellness, *11*(3), 67-82.

https://doi.org/10.1016/j.ijsw.2022.03.004

Lewis, M. (2022). Whistle-blowers *in the hotel industry: Risks and consequences. Ethics and Compliance Journal, 8*(2), 34-49. Retrieved from https://www.ethicsandcompliancejournal.com

Marriott International. (2022). *Marriott's Commitment to Clean.* Retrieved from https://clean.marriott.com/

Miller, D. (2021). *The illusion of luxury: Hotel spa marketing strategies. Marketing Today, 28*(5), 77-89. Retrieved from https://www.marketingtoday.com

Miller, S. (2021). *The hidden costs of hotel amenities: An insider's view. Consumer Reports, 52*(6), 34-41. Retrieved from https://www.consumerreports.org

Miller, S. (2022). *Room service pricing: What you need to know. Hotel Management Today, 28*(4), 112-118. Retrieved from https://www.hotelmanagementtoday.com

Nelson, K. (2023). *Getting the best value from hotel spa packages.* Hospitality Review, *45*(2), 183-196. https://doi.org/10.1108/HR-12-2022-0487

Patel, A. (2023). *Special offers at hotel spas.* Travel Insights, *32*(4), 88-102. https://doi.org/10.1016/j.tij.2023.03.007

Reynolds, K. A. (2021). *Microbial contamination in hotel rooms: A microbiological perspective.* Journal of Environmental Health, *83*(6), 10-15. Retrieved from https://www.jehonline.org

Robinson, L. (2022). *Loyalty programs and spa discounts.* Journal of Loyalty and Reward Studies, *27*(3), 145-160. https://doi.org/10.1016/j.jlrs.2022.04.002

Skift. (2022). *The real cost of hotel room service: An analysis.* Retrieved from https://www.skift.com

Smith, A. (2022). *The impact of technology on guest experiences in the hotel industry.* International Journal of

Hospitality & Tourism Management, 37(2), 78-91. https://doi.org/10.1016/j.ijhm.2022.01.005

Smith, J. (2020). *Hotel Room Germ Study. TravelMath.* Retrieved from https://www.travelmath.com

Taylor, M. (2022). *Hidden fees in hotel spa services. Travel Weekly, 47*(1), 34-45. Retrieved from https://www.travelweekly.com

Taylor, M. (2022). *Minibar mischief: How hotels sneak charges onto your bill. Travel Weekly, 45*(1), 89-97. Retrieved from https://www.travelweekly.com

Taylor, R. (2021). *How to avoid baggage storage fees at hotels. Budget Travel, 19*(5), 39-45. Retrieved from https://www.budgettravel.com

Thompson, K. (2020). *Hidden hotel fees: What to watch out for and how to avoid them. Traveler's Guide, 12*(8), 58-65. Retrieved from https://www.travelersguide.com

Unite Here. (2021). *Survey of hotel workers: Sexual harassment and safety concerns.* Retrieved from https://www.unitehere.org

University of California, Berkeley Labor Center. (2021). *Musculoskeletal injuries in the hospitality industry: A comprehensive study.* Retrieved from https://laborcenter.berkeley.edu

Williams, B. (2021). *Legal tools for employee silencing: The role of NDAs in hospitality.* Journal of Labor and Employment Law, 36(2), 59-77. https://doi.org/10.1016/j.jlel.2021.04.002

Williams, B. (2023). *Facility fees at hotel spas: What you need to know.* Journal of Hospitality and Tourism Management, 31(2), 98-109. https://doi.org/10.1016/j.jhtm.2023.01.002

World Travel & Tourism Council. (2021). *Economic impact report 2021.* Retrieved from https://www.wttc.org

AFTERWORD

As you close the pages of "The Hotel Conspiracy," I hope you feel empowered with newfound knowledge about the hospitality industry. This journey has been one of revelation and understanding, shedding light on the complexities that often remain unseen during our hotel stays.

Throughout this exploration, we've uncovered the truth behind hotel pricing strategies, cleanliness practices, and the impact of hidden fees. We've delved into the ethical dilemmas facing the industry and explored how transparency can shape a more accountable future.

But this book is not just about exposing secrets, it's about empowering you, the traveller. Armed with this knowledge, you can now navigate your hotel experience with confidence. Whether you're booking your next stay or advocating for change, your awareness can drive meaningful improvements in the hospitality landscape.

Remember, your choices matter. By supporting hotels that prioritise transparency and integrity and by advocating for fair practices, you contribute to a hospitality industry that truly serves its guests with honesty and respect.

Thank you for embarking on this journey with me. Together, let's continue to demand transparency, champion fairness, and ensure that every hotel stay reflects the standards we deserve as travellers.

Safe travels,

Zera Schmidt

www.ingramcontent.com/pod-product-compliance
Lightning Source LLC
Chambersburg PA
CBHW071930210526
45479CB00002B/614